Seeing the Sacred in the Ordinary:
Inspirational Poems of Love, Memory, Light, Hope

Mary F. Lenox

Compilation Copyright © 2023
TBL Publishers
San Diego, CA

Copyright © Mary F. Lenox 2023

All rights reserved.

Printed and bound in the United States of America.

No part of this book may be reproduced or utilized in any form or by any means, electronic or mechanical, including photocopying, recording, or by any information storage or retrieval system, except by a reviewer who may quote brief passages in a review to be printed in a magazine or newspaper, without permission in writing from the publisher. Inquiries should be emailed to Mary F. Lenox at mflenox69@gmail.com

First Printing, August 2023

ISBN 979-8-218-20102-9

LCCN: 2019911404

Book Design: Lynn Winston/Powell Graphics & Communication

Color Photos by Mary F. Lenox

> "My destination is no longer a place, rather a new way of seeing."
> - Marcel Proust

My poetry is about seeing the sacred in everyday life.
A poem might begin with a thought, a feeling, a touch, a smell.
A sound, an "Aha!" moment that ignites my imagination.
It's a grace moment. In life there are infinite sacred moments.
Sights, sounds, here, there, everywhere, reveal the divine in plain sight.

Stop

Look

Listen

Feel

Spirit invites you and me to pay attention to sacred moments.
It's the way to connect to the source of creation in the journey of life.

Mary F. Lenox
2023

ACKNOWLEDGMENTS

Thanks to Kelly Alexander, Loretta Brown, Ruby Dancy, Shirley J. Macklin, Suzanne Mahmoodi, and Janice Steinberg for their steadfast love, encouragement, and support.

Table of Contents

Love — 1

Stillness	2
Wake Up to Love	3
Love in Plain Sight	4
Gratitude	5
In the Garden of Gratitude	6
Gratitude in These Times	7
Joy	8
In These Pandemic Times	9
Orbit of Appreciation	11
Fountain of Love	12
Ode to Love	13
About Spirit	14
Oneness of Breath	15
Breath of Life	16
A New Song	17
Rhythm of Life	18
Divine Embrace	19
Come Home	20
Choose Peace	21
Fresh Grace	22
Simple Pleasures	23
Hold on to Love	24

Wanderings	25
Give Thanks Anyway	26
Freedom	27

Memory — 29

The Picture	30
One	32
Story of Juneteenth	33
Her Journey	35
The Majestic Sea	38
I Can't Breathe	39
Flavors of Grace	41
Day of Remembrance	43
Signs of the Times	45
Constant Change	46
It's A Revelation	47
A Gift of Grace	49
In the Land of the Free and Home of the Brave	50
The Story of the Beachcomber	52
A Memorial Tribute	53
Beyond Death	55
Kitchen Table Blues	56
The Mathematician and the Poet	59
In Praise of Trees	61
Grief Stories	63
Father, Forgive Them …	65

We Are One	67
Seasons	69
Year-End Gratitude	71

Light

	73
Come Into the Light	74
Journey Within	75
Just Being	76
Common Ground	77
Lean Into the Light	78
Precious Moment	79
Light and Darkness	80
Just Beyond	81
The Gaze of the Sun	82
The Forever Gift	83
Tender Morn	84
Colors of Life	85
Look for the Light	86

Hope

	87
The Great Migration	88
The Gift of Hope	91
Remembrance	93
Baltimore Riot	94
Still, We Hope	95

Nature's Model of Hope	97
The Web	98
Only a Look	99
Born Again	100
Contrasts	101
Artistic Journey	102
The Sunflowers	103
Blue	104
Lesson of the Morning	105
Hope Endures	106
Sacred Pause	108
Hold On to Hope	109
Perfect Trust	110
Gifts of Grace	111
The Author	113

Love

Stillness

Mission Bay waters
Still as a pristine mountain lake
Await new dawn

Amid orange glow
Bright orb of life
Silently ascends into clear blue sky

My heart smiles with blissful adoration
For heavenly light adorning the atmosphere
In dazzling beauty

I walk along the shore
Listening to divine Spirit whisper:

Taste and see
    The magnificent gift of light
        Embracing you with love
            In the stillness of now!

Wake Up to Love

Wake Up to Love
Welcome the dawn
With a joyful, hopeful heart

Wake Up to Love
See the radiant sun smiling at you
From infinite space

Wake Up to Love
Inhale the fragrance of new life
With every breath

Wake Up to Love
Adorn yourself with courage
To be your authentic self

Wake Up to Love
Dance, sing, praise
Let your spirit rejoice

Wake Up to Love
Receive the gift of peace
In oceans of love

**Wake Up to Healing Love
NOW!**

Love in Plain Sight

See love
Revealed in sacred moments
Of ordinary life

Feel the love of a stranger
Welcoming you into her heart
With a smile

Celebrate the kindness of your friend
Who knows you from the inside out
Accepting you just as you are

Witness endangered monarch butterflies
In flights of hope
Pollinating flowers for future fruits and vegetables

Hear the magnificent rhythms of the sea
Fulfilling its purpose of life-giving oxygen for you, me
All life on planet Earth

Savor the fragrance of Georgia peaches
Ripe with sweetness
For that birthday cobbler

Sing a song of gratitude for love
That divine spirit of the universe
Free to all, just like the stars

Gratitude

In an atmosphere where rudeness is too common
Retreat from civility has become the normal
Gratitude is the way
To live a tender life of compassion and care

Gratitude and gratefulness are one
Like two peas in a pod in a shared space
Affirming
Separateness yet togetherness

Kindness is an aspect of gratefulness
A single act of kindness benefits both
The giver and receiver

Gratitude is an aspect of love
Flowing from the heart
With joyful appreciation for the blessings of our lives

Gratefulness emerges from the deep reservoir of gratitude
With a smile, an acknowledgment
It's seeing the sacred in the ordinary things of life

What if we lived in a world of grateful people
Caring for each other and all life as a practice of love
Would it be paradise on Earth?

In the Garden of Gratitude

She walked in the garden of gratitude
Whispering a hymn of praise
Picking blossoms of kindness blooming all around

She strolled along rows of elegant pink roses
Gazing at her
With smiling faces

Their intoxicating aroma
Inviting her to linger
For a while

She looked toward the heavens
Grateful for the sun in an azure sky
Touching her with dazzling light

She tasted the sweetness of morn
Like butterflies sipping nectar from flowers
Without a care

She savored precious moments
Thankfulness grows in her heart
Awakening her to divine love

Gratitude in These Times

A year of global challenges
Like none other, yet
Life continues
I am grateful

The sun is there
Rising beyond the horizon
This new day of bountiful blessings
I am grateful

Gentle morning breeze
Touching my face with love
Ignites my spirit with a song of praise
I am grateful

Those orange blooms
Surrounded by ruby red bougainvillea
Invite my gaze to their beauty
I am grateful

The sea roars to shore
Endlessly giving life
In waves of relentless change
I am grateful

Joy

Oh, joy!
The glory of the morning
Aglow in heavenly light

Oh, joy!
The blessing of the golden sun
Beaming to planet Earth

Oh, joy!
Splendor of azure sky
Echoing hallelujah, hallelujah, hallelujah

Oh, joy!
The rhythmic bliss of the sea
Dancing to the speed of life

Oh, joy!
Wondrous joy
Welcoming our souls to the banquet of love

In These Pandemic Times

Yesterday
They closed the beaches and the bays
Now I need to make a new plan
To look at sunrise and sunset, from afar

Yet the sun is there
Welcoming me into the light
 Just like love
  Throughout the day

Memories of the sun
Soothe my spirit
I know it is there
Cloudy skies or not

That's trust
Holding me close
Like caressing warmth on a
Sunny summer day

It's time to banish fear fueled by
Inner turmoil
Fake news and truth
In the same pot

Spirit speaks:

Call forth peace
Welcome hope into your heart
Right here, right now

*Find ways to encourage yourself
Sing along with Carrie Newcomer
"You Can Do This Hard Thing"*

*Surrender to the moment
Lean into grace
Receive the gift of love*

Orbit of Appreciation

I wish I could say that it is all about you
It is not
It is all about me

Answering the call of generosity
That sparks my authentic self to give
Straight from my heart to yours

When I do this
My heart smiles
My body wants to leap for joy

I want your heart to smile too
Just like mine
Even if that doesn't happen

I have shared the gift of love
Blessing you and me
Anyhow!

Fountain of Love

Come

To the fount of love

Linger

For a while

Drink

From the well of joy

Rest

In stillness of peace

Allow

The flow of love to be the essence of you

Ode to Love

The search for love

Begins from within

With full acceptance

Of all parts

Unconditionally

Completely

Wholly

Regardless

Then

You will receive

That which is there

Awaiting your embrace

About Spirit

Where is Spirit?
Is it there?
In waves of the sea
Anointing the shore
Again and again

Is it there?
Amid the hazy sky
White as gray fog
Slowly floating in the wind
On an early autumn morn

Is it there?
Offering unconditional love
To all life
In an eternal flow of grace
Everywhere

Is it there?
In solar systems
Galaxies
Planets, Universe

Is it there?
As alpha and omega
Wondrous Spirit
Relentless creator
Sacred light

I say Yes! Yes! Yes!

Oneness of Breath

You were there before the beginning of time
A divine gift of life
An eternal flow of grace
To planet Earth

Earthlings
Offer prayers, chants, songs, breathwork
In humble adoration
Of your sacred healing power

You are everywhere
In the air we breathe
In ocean waves, high and low
In seaweed resting on the sandy shore

I inhale and exhale you
Feeling your vibrations in me
Ever mindful, without you, the world wouldn't exist

Praise be to the breath of love
An omnipresent miracle
Uniting all beings as ONE!

Breath of Life

There is an invisible Spirit
Beyond skin and bone
Within me and you
Wherever we may roam

I live by that presence
The source of all there is
Filling me with love
Breath by breath

The space between
Inhaling and exhaling
Offers a moment of stillness
Inviting rest in the arms of faith

Some day
When I breathe my last breath on planet Earth
I will journey onward into the mystery
Free of worldly circumstances

I whisper a song of gratitude
For the glorious breath of life
Renewing my body, mind, spirit
Here and now

A New Song

Early light did not linger
Gloomy May grays
Thick as sheep wool
Shroud the heavens
Into the afternoon

How to rise above it all
When dark clouds hang so low
Remember to be grateful
No matter how it seems
Dimness can't touch peace within

Sing a new song of love
Welcome this day
Of fresh hope
Just as it is
In this moment

Rhythm of Life

There are as many ways to dance

As there are people dancing

There are as many songs to sing

As there are singers

There are as many ways to love

As there are grains of sand on the shore

So just start where you are

And

Keep dancing, singing, and loving

Divine Embrace

> *All beings are words of God. His music, His art.*
> *- Meister Eckhart (c.1260-1328)*

Gentle bay waves kiss the sandy shore
Like invisible wind
Anointing my skin

Half-moon in a blue sky
Gaze at yonder sunrise
Refreshing the atmosphere with adoring light

No doubt about this gift of love
Restoring, renewing, invigorating, healing
Land, sea, you, me

Love is God's way
Of offering a loving embrace to all beings
In the oneness of life

I receive love with an open heart
On my journey
Into the mystery of change

Come Home

Come home to Spirit
That gift of life given at birth
Ever restoring body, mind, spirit
Breath by breath

Come home to Spirit
Pause, listen
Inhale the fragrance
Of a fresh dawn

Come home to Spirit
See blue sky smiling at you
Celebrate with a song of gratitude
Be thankful for it all

Come home to Spirit
Invite your imagination
To soar from the depth
Of your being

Come home to Spirit
Awaken your heart
To love
Now!

Choose Peace

Get comfortable with change
That is where healing begins
Allow your life to flow
Just as it is
Knowing that each moment
Will never come again
Love yourself enough
To choose peace
In the midst of change

Fresh Grace

Surfers in the mighty sea
Pause
In the hope of catching high waves of morn
For moments of pure bliss

I stand on the boardwalk
Breathing the breath of life
Invigorating my body, mind and spirit
With delightful ease

Clear blue sky reflects
On azure sea
Pulsating at the speed of sound
In brilliant light

I continue on my way
Singing a song of gratitude
Thankful for fresh grace
Inviting my soul to rest in the arms of love

Simple Pleasures

Wake Up!
Kiss night dreams goodbye

Smile at nature's gifts
Glowing in the sun

Inhale the aroma of love
Welcoming you into a new life

Listen to the chirping birds
In a chorus of praise

See morning glory rising
As the brightest star gazing at planet Earth

Inhale the breath of divine love
Renewing body, mind, and spirit, 20,000 breaths per day

Listen to Spirit within
Resounding rhythms of eternity

Rejoice with a heart of gratitude
Receive fresh grace today

Live in the glow of love
Always loving you!

Hold on to Love

Hold on to love
The divine spirit animating all life

Hold on to love
The essence of creativity, imagination, joy

Hold on to love
Revealed in worlds of flora, fauna, humanity

Hold on to love
In the darkest night and brightest light

Hold on to love
Amid struggle, pain, danger

Hold on to love
Healer of the world

Hold on to love
The alpha and omega of infinite grace

Hold on to love
Through kindness, patience, faith, hope, courage

Hold on to love
The light, regardless of temporal circumstances

Hold on to love
With an open heart and relentless gratitude

Hold on to love
Breath by breath

Wanderings

A posse of pelicans
Fly low over the sea in tranquil ease
Oblivious of brown, red, and green seaweed
Resting on the beach

I wonder
Where has the seaweed been?
What has it seen, touched, or heard?
Riding the waves of change

Where will the sea plants go?
When high tides
Carry them back into the ocean
On their voyage into the mystery

The journeys of seaweed
So reminiscent of life
Fraught with unknowns, vicissitudes of highs and lows
Sunny skies, dark nights

Yet, we are never alone
When we embrace love
Forever with us
On our journey home

Give Thanks Anyway

Scant light barely seen amid gloomy gray billows
Give thanks anyway

Rippling bay waves with no place to go
Give thanks anyway

Spring seems asleep in the chilly morn of May
Give thanks anyway

A restless mind clings to discordant thoughts
Give thanks anyway

A garden of succulents awaits the gaze of appreciation
Give thanks anyway

Spirit whispers:
Give thanks anyway, anywhere, anyhow
For all creation with a heart of gratitude
Lifting spirits to the higher ground of love

Freedom

I sing because I am free
Free to be me
For I finally know freedom is from within

My enslaved ancestors
Endured sorrow, terror, and pain for centuries without pay
Bought, sold, dehumanized for money, power, greed
After the Civil War, economic bondage ruled the day

They tried to take my freedom from me
With miseducation, neglect, ghetto life, religious justification
That would not be
For I discovered

Freedom is a state of mind
Wrapped up in my bones
And that is the way it will be

Look at me
I am free, can't you see?
Because of the gift of love

Stop
Look
Listen

Discover divine love within **thee** and be

FREE!
FREE!
FREE!

Memory

Photo (left)
My father, Eleazar Lenox (top row, left), and to his right, siblings Jessie Lenox and James C. Lenox, on bottom row (left) his sister Violet Lenox, (right) his sister, Zephyr Lenox; and (center) their father, Stephen Lenox.

Photo (right)
Eleazar and Truesillia Bryson Lenox on their Wedding Day, April 2, 1936

The Picture

Who are these people?
Who took a leap of faith
To journey to the "promised land"
During the great migration of African American people

Who are these people?
Defined as nobodies (by some)
Held hostage by systemic oppression
And unabashed racism
Refusing to surrender their souls
To the darkness of ghetto life

Who are these people?
Who found an oasis of hope
Through a fervent belief in God
And "loving thy neighbor as thyself"

Who are these people?
Courageously facing the unknown
Day by day, deed by deed
Sharing their life of service and love

Who are these people?
Daring to begin again, again, and again
Through joys and sorrows, despair and struggle
Lifting their hearts in prayer

Who are these people?
Who inspired their children and so many others
To learn, to dream, to create, to grow
Regardless of obstacles and setbacks

Who are these people?
Who left their legacy of love and hope in my heart
These are they!
My ancestors!

One

*If we have no peace, it is because we have
forgotten that we belong to each other.*
- Mother Teresa

Imagine
A world where people everywhere
Awaken to the common bond of "we-ness"
Fauna, flora, humanity, land, and sea
Ally and kin in the unity of oneness

Imagine
One global community
In a cocoon of loving-kindness, compassion, friendship
Would we have issues of climate change, divisive politics, wars,
Class, gender, race, cultural divides?

Imagine
Planet Earth
Connecting humanity with "we-ness" by thought, word, deed
Celebrating gratitude
Every day

Imagine
A cosmos
Where peace, unity, love
Are as ubiquitous as light
What would that world be like?

Imagine
Choosing to be in oneness with life
On the common ground of love
Loving others like God loves all

Story of Juneteenth

Tick-tock
Tick-tock
Tick-tock

Waiting
Waiting
Waiting

Rumors whispered and lingered
That President Abraham Lincoln
Had signed the Emancipation Proclamation
To free all enslaved people in Confederate States

Those enslaved and shackled people in Texas wondered,
"Why aren't we free?"
Following two long years of waiting for their freedom,
The message came on June 19, 1865

2000 Union soldiers marched into Galveston, Texas
Announcing to 250,000 Black people
They were freed by executive decree

Hopeful celebrations erupted with songs, dancing, prayers
Yet, many remained on plantations in economic bondage.
In agreements with landowners, they became sharecroppers
In a new oppressive system

Unfortunately, after paying off debt to landowners for using land, seeds, tools, mules, and shacks, countless formerly enslaved people had insufficient food to last through winter.

In remembrance of that great day of liberation
Juneteenth became an annual day to celebrate
Freedom!
Emancipation!
Liberation!

Her Journey

My mother, Truesillia Bryson Lenox

There it was
A single hibiscus bloom
Happily waving to me as I walked by
Its petals
Yellow as the skin of a banana
Delicate as the wings of a butterfly
Slightly wrinkled edges
Revealing hints of goodbye
Body bowing toward the inevitable
A stout stem
Willingly supporting the journey
From bud to fullness
This delicate blossom
Beckoned memories of my mother
As a flower
Slowly fading before my very eyes over time

From the elegant beauty of youth
Into the weariness of the blues
Honed in the flames of forgotten dreams
Despite pain and grief
She saw the light
In her daily meditation
Welcoming her to the haven of rest
She was faithful as the sun to her hour-long practice
Nothing could deter her
From her solo journey into the spirit realm
Her appointment with God
A childhood mystery to me
In hindsight
I realize she was saving her life
Dipping into divine grace
Seeking that spark for the day
Like that yellow flower
Reaching for the light
A miracle awaits
For that flower lasting only a day
Another bud on the way
Of this wondrous plant
Offering hope for a future bloom
Now I see
It was waving goodbye
Just like my mother
In her own way
She
Carefully selecting the hospital
When I overheard her say
"The Swedish Covenant Hospital
Has a nice Christian name"

A light bulb flashed in my mind
She is choosing where she is going to die!
I felt a reluctant acceptance
As my heart cried with dismay
Mom never returned home
Three weeks later
She was gone
Gladly speaking her final farewells
To her family, saying
"Let me go, let me go"
Soon
She peacefully answered the call
Come home!

The Majestic Sea

> *With every drop of water you drink, every breath you take, you're connected to the sea. No matter where on Earth you live.*
> *- Sylvie Earle*

After the chill of morn
Autumn sunlight
Soothes my body with delight like a summer gift

Not a cloud in the sky
As a quartet of pelicans
Fly above the Pacific with joyful glee

I pause to inhale the fragrant sea
Resounding a rhythmic harmony
Like the beat of my heart
In sweet surrender to each moment

I adore the sea
Day after day, offering life's magnificent treasures
Free to all
Just like divine love

I Can't Breathe

The words said
Written on a waste container
Near the sidewalk
I can't breathe

I wondered
What other
Unheard voices say
I can't breathe

Dying fish of the sea navigating through
Plastic and oil invaders
Echo
I can't breathe

Birds
Call out
Through polluted air
I can't breathe

Children playing
In urban streets
For lack of space elsewhere
I can't breathe

Rivers and streams
Full of sewage from earthlings
Scream
I can't breathe

People of color seek relief from all of the ways oppressors
Try to kill, destroy, eliminate
Shout
I can't breathe

Yet, we will not stand silently
Hearing those words
Day by day
I can't breathe

Now
Young and old around the world
March and proclaim
No more!

Flavors of Grace

She was always in the kitchen
Serving a home-cooked breakfast
Fried apples, scrambled eggs, hot biscuits
Made from scratch

The dough rolled out with an old rolling pin
Onto a white cloth sprinkled with flour
Then carefully cut into rounded circles
Using the top of a small glass

Baked to a crusty golden brown
Warm and ready to eat with butter and jelly
The delicious aroma ignited my taste buds
In a burst of delight

Soon

She would begin preparing dinner
A daily feast worthy of a royal celebration
Fried chicken, mustard, and turnip greens
Candied yams

Other times, slow-roasted beef with veggies
Always homemade cornbread
With just a pinch of sugar
(To bring out the flavor, she said)

No written recipe did she ever use
In creating her delicious food
Dessert, the grand finale,
Sweet potato pie

Her cooking was a love affair
With expertise born of passion
Although she could neither read nor write
She gladly shared her recipes

Passed down orally
From generation to generation
In memories of families and friends
Her name was Mary

We called her Aunt Honey
Her steadfast faithfulness to her culinary art
A practice of kindness, love, generosity, grace
Cooking was her cocoon of happiness

Although she left this world decades ago
Her sweet spirit lives in my heart as a flame of joy
Thank you, Aunt Honey
Thank you!

Day of Remembrance

There
In morning light
A tiny leaf
Slowly falls to the ground
Whispering its final goodbye
To await transformation beyond sight
That leaf and Queen Elizebeth II
Whose funeral was celebrated on September 19, 2022
Saying farewell
Both entering into the mystery
Joining others
Rich, poor, high, low
Male, female
Plants, animals
All
Sooner or later
Passing beyond earthly matters into the infinite realm
Hundreds at Westminster Abbey
Joined millions around the world
To say farewell to the 93-year-old monarch
I, the only one, pausing to watch the solo leaf falling
Death of a queen, the demise of a leaf
Offer a powerful lesson

Celebrate life
Love
Work
Play
Be real
Be grateful
Live to the fullest
NOW

Any day
Any moment
Any second
Might be the last chance to say yes to life

Signs of the Times

Seaweed on the beach reveals
High tide has come and gone
Leaving behind its bountiful gifts
Vacation rentals and hotels stand empty
As landlords sing the blues
Hoping for the end to the pandemic

Call of that blackbird claiming its territory and
Shorebirds seeking nourishment
Tell bird tales of morn
Cyclists, runners, walkers
Do their morning rituals in the alley
Rather than the boardwalk
The ordinary and the extraordinary
Both exist in real-time
Life goes on-pandemic or not!

Constant Change

Change is the only constant in life.
- Heraclitus, Greek Philosopher

In tranquil atmosphere

Rippling bay water welcomes daybreak

I pause to gaze at the ascending sun

Gradually becoming fully visible on the horizon

Suddenly

As if struck by a jolt of lightning

Turbulent water surges with fierce ferocity

Then returns to calmness

Isn't that like life?

Serenity is replaced by spirals of anxiety in a blink

Uncertainty prevails over enjoyment

As currents of change become

Waves of doubt, fear, sadness

Nevertheless

With faith, hope, and courage as my partners

I look for peace in my heart

Regardless of what's going on

For change is the variable

That keeps life moving

Regardless of earthly circumstances

It's A Revelation

Fear
The mother of darkness
Married deception
They bore children
Naming them
Anger
Hatred
Sadness
Ego
Selfish
Spiteful
Machiavelli
Narcissism
Envy
Greed
The family lived together in the wilderness called darkness

One day
As if from another world
Brilliant beams of light appeared echoing

Come
I AM
Hope

Come
I AM
Courage

Come
I AM
Faith

Come
I AM
Confidence

Come
I AM
Happiness

Come
I AM
Clarity

Come
I AM
Joy

Come
I AM
Peace

Come
I AM
Gratitude

Come
I AM
Love

Soon the family realized they had a choice
Cling to the place of darkness
Or
Be transformed by the light

A Gift of Grace

I have what I want.
I want what I have.
(unknown)

Aunt Frances Edwards shared a small apartment in Chicago
Her tiny bedroom in perfect order
She was watching a Chicago Cubs baseball game
When I arrived, her television was soft enough for us to talk

I asked her
"Do you need anything?"
She answered, "No, I like baseball; I am watching it.
I like pork; it is in the refrigerator.
I like ice cream; it's in the freezer."

At that moment
My great-aunt taught me a powerful lesson
About contentment
No envy, no regret, no unhappiness
Living a simple life of being content with what she had

Later in life
She would gift me her precious possessions
Before her final goodbye.
Gone for decades, her quiet presence lives in my spirit
Echoing

Open the door to contentment
Know what you need and have it
Be grateful
Receive the gift of peace

In the Land of the Free and Home of the Brave

While at Marshall Fields, founded in Chicago in 1852,
Renowned for its then high-quality merchandise,
I remember answering "yes" to a question by the
   white salesperson

My mother immediately said to me,
Say, "Yes, ma'am."
At that moment, I wondered in my young mind
If my mother was teaching me my place in the scheme of things

Decades later
At an upscale suburban store
I noticed a cape with a leopard print design and a matching hat
I asked the white salesperson the price

She didn't answer my question but immediately replied
"A cheaper one is over there"
Did she think I couldn't pay for the one I desired
Because I was a Black woman?

I bought the expensive cape
In spite of her assumptions
Until this day
The bittersweet memory of that encounter
Lingers

I walked into a neighborhood hair supply store in Chicago
Without a word of welcome
The Asian proprietor said
"Leave your packages here in the front"

I said, "Do you think I'm going to steal something?"
I walked out without purchasing anything
Vexed by the notion that he earned a living
Insulting Black customers showing up to shop

Fear gripped me as I drove weekly to Springfield, Missouri
Returning home on dark, remote highways
With lots of twists and turns
I prayed that I wouldn't have a police encounter and
Disappear into the fog of the criminal justice system

Countless incidents throughout my life
Remind me of the dark side of being Black
In the land of the free and home of the brave

On this new day of new beginnings
Divine light between coal-gray clouds
Inspires my heart to keep the flame of hope alive
In my heart
No matter what

The Story of the Beachcomber

There she was
Pulling a large wagon across the sandy beach
An overflowing cargo of discarded blankets, towels, and toys
Can seem so heavy, yet, she carried on.

She worked with zeal
Picking up discarded trash
Then pausing to look at me
Asking, "Are you all right?" I said, "Yes."

I asked, "What do you do with all of that stuff?"
Her answer surprised me
Explaining how she washed the dirty towels and toys to donate
Giving the cans to some homeless guys to sell

She counted each piece with pride, saying
"I've picked up 1400 pieces so far today, counting caps
And thousands more this year
It's all about moving the body while caring for the sea."

Kathy, the beachcomber
Turning trash into gems of generosity
On her divine mission of care for herself, the ocean, and others
Everyday

Praise be to Kathy
Following the wisdom of her heart while serving the planet
Day by day
Amazing!

A Memorial Tribute

Loyal, trustworthy, creative, no-nonsense
These are the words that come to mind when
I think of my dear niece, Truesillia.
She always had your back, often quietly working in the
background to help you achieve your goals. Her ever-present
commitment to serving the needs of family and friends
was her call. If she agreed to assist you, you could take her
commitment to the bank.

I remember calling to read a draft of my poem to ask her opinion
about using a particular word; she stopped whatever she was
doing and listened carefully and attentively, then shared her ideas
with me. In addition, she used her extensive computer skills when
I needed her to help me with projects. She always made me feel
loved and appreciated. She took the time to talk with me and
reflected her kindness by being ready to assist me and others in
any way possible.

She was ever mindful of her mother's needs.
Most likely, if you saw her mother, Trueannie Oaddams,
Truesillia was nearby, especially in later years.
They were not only mother and daughter but also companions,
buddies, and devoted friends in the journey called life.

After our parents passed away, our family reunions were often in
restaurants and banquet halls or at the home of the Oaddams.
Truesillia was the backbone of the extensive planning and
execution of this long standing family tradition.
Remarkably, in the last year of her life, she insisted on preparing
the entire Thanksgiving dinner as her special gift of love to us.

Truesillia helped our family stay connected through calls and
other ways of acknowledging our common bond.
Her abundant creativity was rich with colorful expressions,
powerful insights, and humor.

Thanks be to God for the years she was with us and
her gifts of service; her steadfast faithfulness to God, family,
friends, and community will be missed.
Now that her work on this Earth is done, the Master says
"Come Home!"
So she did.

Truesillia Williams: Feb 25, 1963 - Dec 5, 2017
Chicago, Illinois

Beyond Death

My father passed away in silence
Not a word spoken during his last days on Earth
In a coma
Struggling to breathe until the last breath

I wondered:
What did he want to say?
Forever left unsaid
What did he want to do?
Now that his life on Earth is done?

What dreams deferred would he have hastened to fulfill?
Knowing it would be over so soon
What did he still hold close to his heart?
Dreams waiting beyond the robe and roles of his life

Did he hear the whispering call to come to the other side?
Did he believe as I believe
When the battle of the body is over
His spirit still lives in the eternity of God

Kitchen Table Blues

Her life was in the kitchen except when going to bed
Or praying by the steam radiator in the dining room
Warmed by that delicious warmth
Banishing winter's chill

Her side of the kitchen table
A tiny space for her impromptu office
Of pencils, brown bags, whatever
Used to write her "to-do list."

My father's place
The opposite side, with a table setting and chair
Waiting for the 4 pm call
To invite him to come to dinner

Her entertainment
A small radio playing
News, views, and music all day long
From Moody Radio

Her kitchen companions
A stove, sink, table, cabinet, pantry and
Potbelly stove as backup heat in the kitchen
To hold back Chicago's frigid weather

She was always in the kitchen
When I returned from school
Her loving presence was enough to soothe my mind and spirit
I was happy just being with her

Looking back
I realize her sadness
Permeated the house
In a silent aura of grief

Now
My view of her life has changed
I see her as a woman of sorrow enduring hard times
Never healing from her mother's death

She
Age fourteen when her mother died
In her 30s
A victim of Chicago's brutal winters

At age 25, I left home and got my apartment
To find my way in the world
Leaving behind my mother
Who couldn't accept my decision

I left with no regrets
A year later
She said, "I would go too,
If I could do so."

I wonder
Why do memories of my mother's life matter to me now?
Now I know
I have been profoundly affected by my mother's grief

Understanding my mother's life helps me to embrace
Love and compassion
For her, for others, for myself
For the world

Praise be to my mother, Truesillia Bryson Lenox
Who showed me patience, kindness, wisdom, courage
I am eternally grateful for her light of love
Living in my heart

The Mathematician and the Poet

There we were
Sharing common ground of purpose and discovery
on Zoom

He
The mathematician
Fascinated with the language of mathematics
With its symbols, precision, logic

I
The poet
Immersed in the world of imagery
Metaphors, similes, allusions, thoughts, feelings, reflections

He
Young enough to be my grandson
Illuminating with patience, respect, kindness
My understanding of how to organize my poetry
in digital space

I
An elder in my seventh decade of life
Learning new skills on a shared screen of "show and tell"

We
Bridging the gap of age, generation, experience, expertise

I
Thankful for his wisdom
Receiving his generous support, tender loving care
And thoughtful clarity

He
So at ease with his guidance and gift of service

We
Wrapped in a cocoon of shared humanity
In the oneness of divine grace

In Praise of Trees

Poets write about you
Scientists seek to understand you
Theologians muse about your divinity
You inspire and delight

You hold the memories of seasons in your body
Some say you embody the history of life
You survive storms, winds, rains, hurricanes, tornadoes
So marvelous are you!

You nourish and protect
Wildlife find shelter in your hidden spaces
You provide highways and dwellings to insects, mammals
Cambium, sapwood, and heartwood are your kin

Earthlings misuse and abuse you
Burning, chopping, grinding you up
Your body becomes timber
For building houses, bridges, furniture

Your essence inspires endless creations
Of spices, medicine, chemicals, paper, clothes, canoes
You are the epitome of strength, endurance, and longevity
Through it all, you keep on growing, adapting, changing

Day after day
You clean the air
You improve health and enrich the soil
Your powerful presence impacts the flow of falling rain

Even in the sunset of your life
You reveal stunning colors, textures, shapes
Please forgive us for taking so much from you
For you deserve no less than our complete love

Thank you for opening my mind
To see you with new eyes
As the goddess you are
I adore you!

Praise be to you, mighty trees of life
Praise be to the creator
For the gift of your abundant generosity

Thank you!
Thank you!
Thank you!

Grief Stories

I did not know I loved her so
Her generous, tender spirit
Invited me into her heart
There
I discovered her love
Pure and simple

She'd show up unexpectedly at my office
Sometimes
Waiting for hours
Until I had time to talk
Her name
Dr. Lois Bryant

I, the teacher
She, the student
Who became my mentor
Supportive, encouraging, reassuring
Helping me to navigate the territory
Of a new town, a new job, a new life

Lois understood what it meant for me
To move from Chicago to a small college town in Missouri
Without family or friends
I had entered into the wilderness of the unknown
Leaving behind a lifetime of emotional support and love
I did not realize what I had done

Lois welcomed me into her family
Sharing her unconditional love
Her steadfast friendship
Infused with tender care
An incredible blessing
At a very vulnerable time in my life

That morning
We talked briefly on the phone
Making plans to get together after work to play cards
Her sister played, Lois did not
But she said, "I'll be with you anyhow."

That afternoon around 4 pm, the call came
Lois, my dear, dear friend
Killed instantly at the age of 34
Her tiny car crushed between two semi-trucks

The news shocked my heart
Like a bolt of electricity
The grief comes and goes
To this very day, 40 years later

Father, Forgive Them ...

I couldn't stand the pain
I wanted to run away from my grief with no place to hide
I carried in my heart a sorrow I had never known

Sadness, more than three decades ago, awakened today
Triggered by the news of the senseless, violent deaths
In Atlanta, Georgia, and Boulder, Colorado

Father, forgive them, for they know not what they do

Families, friends, community
May never get over the grief
Resurrected in the bright light of memory
Receding into forgetfulness until ignited anew
By an event, a thought, a feeling, a picture
A whisper from the past

Sixty years later
I recall the first time I saw my father cry
He had gotten a call notifying him
Of the violent death
Of his beloved brother, James C. Lenox
Killed under mysterious circumstances

Father, forgive them, for they know not what they do

Then I saw a brilliant sun
Ascending into the pristine blue sky
Reminding me of a new beginning
Like faces of radiant green succulents
Looking at me as I walked by
Echoing, I see you; I send love your way

The pulsating sea
Roaring like a mighty lion in Tanzania
Welcomed me
With a rhythmic song of praise
Wave by wave
Endlessly

I received new insights
Revealed in the early morning light
Of joy and sadness
Living together in my emotional space
I whispered a prayer
Of compassion and understanding

Father, forgive them, for they know not what they do

We Are One

In the beginning
Life began in oneness
There were no continents
Nations, cultures, languages
No governments, boundaries, or borders

Eventually

Humans devised ways to separate and divide
By race, gender, nation, customs, religions, class
Social roles, traditions, and beliefs of all kinds
Forgetting that forests burning in the Amazon
Affect the air we breathe in Chicago and elsewhere

It's time to remember
We Are One

Like those trees along the highway
In oneness with the light
Like bees finding nectar from flowers
While fostering new generations in every bite
Each depends on the other
In a symbiotic relationship of oneness

Can ocean waves
Be separated from the sea
Or blue sky
From itself, even on a cloudy day?
I think not

We Are One

Like the white and black keys of a piano
Each functioning as one in the creation of music
Louis Armstrong, John Coltrane, Florence Price
Beethoven, Bach, Mozart, Teng, Makeba, Yo-Yo Ma
Share their unique sounds in the oneness of music

Picasso saw the light of oneness
As he painted African masks
Georgia O'Keeffe and Ansel Adams
Saw the beauty of landscapes in oneness with nature
So, too, Monet

Yes
 We Are One

That oneness is reflected
By thought, word, and deed
That oneness
Lights my world and yours
In peaceful co-existence

We are **One** in Spirit
We are **One** global community caring for the Earth
We are **One** awakened by the omnipresent connection
Of love for each other
No matter what!

Can't you see?

WE ARE ONE!

Seasons

I awaken from
A night of sweet dreams
Renewed by the warmth
Of peace

I smile with gratitude
For a new day of grace
Welcoming me
Into new life

Ominous dark clouds
Hover in silence
While rain sprinkles the landscape
Amid scant light

No doubt about it
Fall is on parade
Marching
To a song of change

Fewer blooming flowers
Leaves drifting to the ground
In colors of orange, red, purple, brown, yellow
Soon winter will reign

I welcome seasonal changes in nature
Yet
My seasons may occur like Chicago's weather
Four seasons in a day

Sometimes I feel optimistic
Bursting with fresh ideas
My creativity blooming like a summer garden
Then harvested with the gifts of insight and wisdom

On the same day
Fear may hijack my joy
The fog of illusions, pain, sadness
Lingering then fading as I embrace the light

Praise Be!

Regardless of the seasons of my life
Wrapped in waves of uncertainty and relentless change
I can choose to practice living in the moment
Empowered with omnipresent love

Forever present!

Year-End Gratitude

I am grateful!

For every breath
For flowers opening to the light and those saying goodbye
For every tree adorned in seasonal dress
For every season of my life
For my ancestors
Who left me a legacy of hope, love, compassion, kindness,
A thirst for knowledge and love of God
For health that enables my body to feel the energy of life
For a curious, open mind inviting me to explore nature
To learn about people, places, and things in this world
For deepening my relationship with my emotions,
Showing me what love, fear, sadness, and joy feel like
For awakening my consciousness to the oneness of all
For omnipresent love
For my senses:
For seeing beauty wherever I go
For feeling my feet as I walk
For receiving sunlight and wind
For sounds of the sea and silent prayers
For hope that inspires me to trust and keep stepping
For the aura of peace that comforts me in all situations
For the love of myself and others with compassion,
    tenderness, and acceptance
For hope that sustains me
For the rich diversity of life

I am grateful!

Light

Sunset Over the Pacific, Mission Beach, California

Come Into the Light

Come into the light
Where love abides
Drink from the fountain of hope
Inhale fragrances of the divine

Come into the light
Where peace welcomes you
And a rainbow, too
Echoing all is well

Come into the light
Wherever you are
Like that tiny green plant
Cleaving to life in a crack of black cement

Come into the light
Breath
      by
           Breath
Come Home!

Journey Within

In my innermost being

Silence

Welcomes me home

No luggage or companions needed

In this space of solitude

Just an open heart and wakeful awareness

My soul invites me to stay awhile

Receiving love

Breath by breath

Just Being

Sunrise ascends beyond dark clouds
Hovering low in yonder sky
Just Being

Scant light awakens the atmosphere
In the luminous glow of love
Just Being

Tranquil bay waters
Reflect silvery sheen
Just Being

Quartet of seagulls
Play "follow the leader" on a sandy beach
Just Being

Red roses
Bloom in perfect harmony with the light
Just Being

Spirit whispers
Create your life mosaic
Just Being
YOU

Common Ground

> *I believed in the fallacy of being alone*
> *Until I experienced the truth.*
> *- Mary F. Lenox*

What we have in common is the oneness of our humanity
We celebrate the birth of a child
We grieve the loss of grandma
We open our hearts to love ourselves and others
Yes
We fear the unknown in a fog of doubt
We fail to see blessings amid disappointments
We forget each moment is precious
We bind ourselves in a web of fear
Yet
I choose to remember the greatest truth
We are never alone
Amid vicissitudes of our lives
For the eternal gift of love is always with us
Like the breath of life
Lifting us to the higher ground of gratitude

Lean Into the Light

Sunrise unseen
This morn of gloomy clouds
With drizzle

I strolled along the way
Listening for a whisper within for a sip of inspiration
To energize my body, mind, spirit

Then I remembered

When you don't see your way clear
And darkness shrouds your mind
Lean into the light for clarity beyond sight

When impatience holds sway
Banish fear right away
Lean into the light of courage

When life surprises you with dissonance
Of this and that
Lean into the light of stillness

When you can't see your way
In darkest night
Lean into the light of hope

When you feel friendless
With a heavy load of despair
Lean into the light of radical self-love

When showers of disappointment
Rain on your spirit
Lean into the light of fresh joy

Precious Moment

There it was
A lone brown pelican in quiet bay water very close to shore
A surprise visitor from the sea

I wondered
Where did it come from?
Where is it going?

We shared a blissful moment
The pelican and me
Welcoming the sunrise

Soon
The regal traveler
Flew into the mystery

I, too, continued on my way
Enjoying the precious gift of peace
In the early morning light

Light and Darkness

Amid daunting darkness
There is the light of hope

Amid shades of anger, sadness, pain
There is the light of healing

Amid lies to self and others cloaked in ferocious fear
There is the light of truth

Amid relentless belief in lack
There is the light of the infinite abundance of grace

Amid loneliness and separation
There is love awakening us to the oneness of all creation

Just Beyond

Showers of blessings
touch the landscape
with wet joy
Sounds of droplets
anointing green
leaves
Beckon my attention
to a nearby cluster of
tiny yellow blossoms
Silently receiving
Raindrops too
Dense clouds shroud
the sky in dimness
Hope illuminates my
heart like a light
From a lighthouse
In an utterly dark sea

Spirit whispers
Stop!
Look!
Listen!
God is transforming
the Earth with new life
Look there
Just beyond the shade
For light!

The Gaze of the Sun

What does the sun see?
Does it see trembling bay waters?
Does it see that capsized boat?
Does it hear the sounds of crows and mourning doves
    claiming territory?
Does it see those birds of paradise, red begonias
    royal purple bougainvilleas reaching for light?
Does it hear the silent prayers of the lady facing the sea
    as white-capped waves roar toward her relentlessly?
Does it see a full moon revolving around the globe
    welcoming the face of God?
Does it see me walking along the seaward path
    hoping for a moment of inspiration?
Does it see my heart dancing
To a touch of love?

The Forever Gift

Fog rests on fallow ground
Asleep for winter dreams
Barren trees along the way
Reach toward the hazy white sky
Fall gone
Winter here
Nevertheless
Flora, fauna, earthlings
Have their ways of surviving change
Receiving an eternal gift from the sun
As the Earth goes around and around
Leaning toward the light

Tender Morn

Light of morn
Soft as a newborn
Brightens the atmosphere

I walk in an aura of warmth
In splendid delight
With every step

A solo hummingbird
Pauses
Savoring nectar from the trumpet vine

Chirping birds in a nearby tree
Tenderly greet each other
In a chorus of sweet tweets

Blessings flow
From nature's gifts
Straight to my heart

Colors of Life

At the horizon

Spectacular golden glow of sunset

Illuminates the west

Its blissful light shines

Between the horizon and gray haze

Widening its grip on the atmosphere

While the sun disappears

Twilight briefly visits

Then bids farewell

Flaming orange, soft blue, and dense gray

Become the fleeting hues of a rainy day

So like life

With its

Joys and sorrows

Changing precipitation

Brief interludes

Varied tones

Happenings

In any given moment of our lives

Look for the Light

When you don't see your way clear
And darkness seems to ambush your mind
Look for the light of clarity

When impatience holds sway
Banish fear right away
Look for the light of courage

When life surprises you
With dissonance of this and that
Look for the light of peace

When you can't see your way
In desperate despair
Look for the light of hope

When you feel friendless, don't weep
Embrace self-love
Look for the light of self-compassion

When disappointment rains on your parade
Sing a song of gratitude
Look for the light of joy

When nothing else will do
Look for the light of divine love within
Always, always with you

Hope

Sunrise over Lake Michigan

The Great Migration

They came

With hope and created possibilities

Travelers

Hundreds of thousands, countless more

One by one

Making the decision

To leave the past for an unknown future

They came from

Alabama, Tennessee, Mississippi, Georgia, North Carolina

South Carolina, Florida

And so many other regions of the South

Looking to embrace new life in the "promised land" of the North

They came to

Detroit, Chicago, New York, Los Angeles, Philadelphia

And many other cities and towns

Mothers, fathers, sisters, brothers

They came

Grandmothers, grandfathers, children, the yet unborn

They came

Uncles, aunts, cousins, nieces, nephews

They came

By train, car, walking

They came

From rural roots

To urban sprawl

They came

Some money, little money, no money

A sandwich

A name or two

Of relatives and friends who had already made the journey

They came

Living in kitchenettes, apartments, church havens

And ghetto spaces beyond imagination

Still

They came

No job, no education

Yet

They came

They

Could not

Would not

Dare not

Turn around

So

They held a prayer in their hearts

And faith that "The Lord will make a way."

Moment by moment

Step by step

Day by day

Connecting to the divine

And each other, with the help of partners

Created schools, churches, communities

Businesses, music, literature, art

Cultural expressions denied for 400 years

All the while

Believing that they could and would create

New lives

From remnants of hope

And so

THEY DID!

The Gift of Hope

There it was on my table
As the Bible of my life entitled
African American Poetry: 250 years of Struggle & Song
Illuminating the fight to survive
In the land of the free and home of the brave

968 pages telling of
Misery, cruelty, hatred, murder
Unimaginable dehumanization
By actions to strip my people of their humanity

The venom continues under the guise of
    "We serve and protect"
Policymakers, enemies, strangers determined to keep
    "Those people in their place"
Justifying relentless oppression with misinformation,
    miseducation, policies, and practices
To keep the greed and profit machine alive and well

People
Stolen from Africa for free labor
Their descendants continue to live
With hope despite relentless oppression

Sometimes
Hope rises and falls
Like the ebb and flow of waves
Ever returning to the oneness of it all

Can't you see
Hope rests
In the oneness of love
Inspiring hearts to carry on

Oh,
May I remember to keep hope
Living in me
Like the light of the sun!

Remembrance

The sun did not forget to rise this dawn

Its radiant glow

Like clockwork

Ascends into blue skies

It did not forget

To anoint the atmosphere

With luminous light

It did not forget

To warm the spirit with fresh hope

 It did not forget

To kiss sparse clouds with brightness

It remembered to do what it does every day

Be a light to the world

Why can't we be like the sun?

Baltimore Riot

Night of rage

Born

Not of yesterday

But for many moons

Festering community sores

Now ruptured

After a murderous incident with police

Another African American male

Dead in the streets

For what or why?

Fires

Fights

Violent destruction

Chaos

Fear

In the darkness of anger

Daylight brings an uneasy calm

Healing Hope

Not yet real

God help us all!

Still, We Hope

Misty, wet fog
Shrouds land and sea
With a milky white aura

People
Erect summer shade covers
Without a speck of sun in sight

A couple walk with their rubber boat
Toward the bay happy as could be
Hoping for a fun Labor Day

I said to them, "I wish I could go."
She said, "I wish I could take you with me."
I said, "Take me in spirit."
We continued our separate ways

Large fishing boat on the river
Moving toward the sea
Towing a smaller one with nets
In hopes of catching tuna

Parking lots full in dim light
Families gather by river, bay, sea
For a piece of peace
Resting, playing, sharing

In the news
Police still killing
Black and Brown people
With vicious intent

Others protest
No more!
Marching
Here and there

Wildfires in California barely contained
Exhausted firefighters fight on
With the aid of helicopters
In hope of defeating the flames

Florence Price, the pioneering African American composer,
Despite daunting societal oppression
And relentless assaults on her failing body,
Created exquisite beauty with her music
Bringing tears to my eyes
As my soul smiles with wondrous joy

Artists of many stripes shout out
Stop!
Look!
Listen!
Inhale!
Exhale!
Feel the love!

Life continues with hope
Wrapped in love

Nature's Model of Hope

Nature is the master teacher of hope
Look at the hummingbird's nest
Hidden among the greens
With two white eggs holding life for the next generation

But wait

Storms, rains, winds, predators, heat, cold
Constant threats to survival
Mother hummingbird protects the nestling's home
With her tiny body
In the hope for chicks to emerge from the eggs

Hatchlings' mouths wide open, waiting for constant feeding
She seeks and hopefully finds food for them
Each day a new challenge from dawn to dusk

One day, mom leaves
The chicks are on their own
Each finding a way
Into the mystery of uncertainty

Isn't that hope?
Entering into the unknown
On the wings of faith
Awake to the miracle

We are never alone
With the gift of divine love
Holding us
In a cocoon of grace

The Web

There it was

Waving in the wind

In the foggy mist

Held in space

By uneven strands

Attached to nameless weeds

Fresh dewdrops

Clinging to its surface

Announcing the presence

Of this mysterious creation

Seeking to entice visitors

To the circle of

Hope and death

Only a Look

There she was
Leaning over the guardrail adjacent to the highway
To look into that lush valley below
Green shrubs, trees, flowers
Perfectly still, receiving moisture from a thin veil of fog

She
Had the wisdom to stop and look
Silently take in the gift of beauty below
As cars roared by

She
Unperturbed by rush hour traffic
The serenity of twilight
Long gone replaced with urban noise

She
Inhales the peace of life looking at the natural world
Taking a sip of the nectar of joy
Right there on the side of the road

My heart smiled
As I looked at the stranger
Who could have been me
I remember to pause, taste and see blessings
In front of my very eyes

Born Again

I thought I'd never see them again
Those wild weeds clinging to earth
With tiny golden yellow blossoms
Reaching for holy light

Yet
There they were
In the quiet calm of morn
Seemingly dead only yesterday
Now born again like the mythological phoenix

I whispered a prayer of hope
Oh!
May I remember to remember
The gift of new life rises
From the ashes of change

Contrasts

Dawn of light

Like cat eyes

Pierces through

Dense black clouds

Silence

Surrenders

To roar of motorists

Rushing to and fro

Darkness fades

Luminous glow

Struggles

To breakthrough

Gloomy haze

Hope rises

In heart

Patiently waiting

For sun

To smile

Artistic Journey

There it was
Like an exquisite painting
Lovingly crafted from found objects and pieces of a dream
A delightful gift of becoming
That giant gourd
Divided into a trio of parts
Reimagined by the artist, Apua Garbutt
In hues of bright yellow flowers
And tones of orange, bronze, and black
Born of faith, imagination, and passion
Standing naked in the world
Mysterious, majestic presence
Whispering messages of femininity, sexuality, birth
Pregnant with possibilities
The artist
Living in hope
Willing to risk it all by cutting it open
Just three days ago
For a chance of singular beauty
Straight from her heart
She answered the call
With focused intent
Offering her joyful creation
Smiling to one and all
Just like the sun!

The Sunflowers

A pot of brilliant sunflowers
In bright sun reached for me as I passed by
Whispering, "Take me home."

My visit to the greenhouse
Enticed me to buy that joyful sunflower plant
Its happy yellow blooms made me smile

The following day a few petals were drooping
Like the skin of an old woman
With edges of white death beneath the yellow hue

A moment of sadness
Zapped my heart
As I realized the inevitable

Yet, tiny buds wrapped in green sleeves
Offered hope for new blossoms
To brighten my someday

Blue

Blue sky of early morn
Reflects the mighty sea
Resounding waves
Like a sweet melody

I stroll along the boardwalk
Envisioning the symbolism of blue
Expansiveness, intuition, imagination, faith, freedom
Is that why people are attracted to that divine hue?

Blues music infused with African rhythms
Born on plantations and in churches of enslaved people
And their descendants
Echo "blues" of pain, death, and sorrow
Living a nightmare of terror and fear
While clinging to hope

I wonder what blues songs tell the stories of
Profound losses from the Covid-19 pandemic?
What are the words that can heal our hearts
As we hope
For deliverance

Lesson of the Morning

There they were at the edge of the bay
A flock of shorebirds
Seeking morsels with focused intent

No doubt, no fear, no procrastination
No time to waste precious moments
Of hope and promise

So, too, that green plant with new buds
Reaching for life beyond the fence
Waiting in silent repose for whatever comes

There on the sidewalk
A tiny trio of rootless red begonias
With unopened buds slowly surrendering to death

Such is life

Like the ebb and flow of the sea
Leaving behind seaweed on the sandy shore
Waiting for the next destination

What to do in this land of endless possibilities?
Give thanks for what is
Blessing your every step

Look for the light of hope
Whatever the season
To illuminate your journey
To newness of life!

Hope Endures

He was wearing a symbol on his shirt
Of a weeping American flag
Dripping in strips of blackness
I wondered why he was attracted to that symbol

Earlier, I felt a deep sadness
Listening to Toni Morrison's description
Of the interior lives of enslaved women
In her incredible prize-winning novel, *Beloved*

Morrison's words ignited my imagination
Zapping my spirit with a lightning bolt of heartbreak
For the millions of enslaved people and their descendants
Enduring untold misery

Nevertheless

I walked along the boardwalk
Watching surfers wade in the blue sea
Waiting to catch the perfect wave
For moments of pure joy

Two seagulls soaring high in the sky
Playing with each other
"Catch me if you can."
As if nothing else mattered

Spider webs among green plants
Still as a windless dawn
Silently echoed hope
For a blessing of nourishment

Solo worker bee
Among purple lavender flowers
Sought the promise of nectar
With faithful ease

People of various ages
Walking, eating, playing, selling merchandise
Continuing in the flow of new life
In their unique ways

In the light of morn, I saw a new vision of hope
Someday, people around the world
Will embrace the unifying power of love
With relentless compassion, kindness, respect

Meanwhile, hope lives in my heart
As I remember the sacred text
"Weeping may endure for a night,
but joy cometh in the morning!"
       Psalms, 30:5 KJV

Sacred Pause

With blessings of grace
In a crescendo of joy
I whisper a prayer

Oh, what a day to breathe the breath of love
Over and over
In praise of this holy day

Remembering
Every time we breathe
God is saying, "I love you."

Hold On to Hope

In the darkest night

Travel lightly

Into the unknown

With awakened faith

Let go of the temptation

To turn back or give up

Just keep walking

Step by step

Toward the light

Ever present

For you!

Perfect Trust

I wonder if raindrops have perfect trust in gravity
Or will doubt keep them suspended
Between Heaven and Earth?

What of yellow flowers in the meadow there
Do they have perfect trust that sunlight will find them?

What is perfect trust?

Is it a baby smiling in the safety of a mother's arms?
Is it a monarch butterfly on wings of hope?

Is it sea waves cycling to shore repeatedly becoming one
In the mystery of change?

Is it humans, flora, fauna?
Blessed by the flow of grace saying "Yes!" to light

Yes!
Yes!
Yes!

I trust in divine guidance and the goodness of life
I trust love, hope, courage, grace, generosity, and patience
As my partners

When death knocks on my door
My body will bid goodbye to planet Earth
I trust in the eternity of love

Forever!
Forever!
Forever!

Gifts of Grace

Clouds meander amid gray sky
Waves of the mighty sea cycle to and fro
Hummingbirds fly in flights of hope
Hibiscus blooms reach for light
Earthlings move at the speed of grace

Yes, indeed
Fauna, flora, all species
Blessed by daily grace
Like manna for enslaved Israelites in ancient Egypt
Like water in dry places of life's circumstances

Oh!
What joy to feast on the beauty of grace
As far as the eyes can see
Grace
A divine gift beyond measure
Straight from the wellspring of love

The Author

Born in Chicago, **Mary F. Lenox** is a writer, poet, and educator. Her career includes serving as a librarian, researcher, and university professor. She earned a certificate of advanced studies from the Chicago Theological Seminary.

For twelve years she served as the first African American dean at the University of Missouri-Columbia. She has traveled to forty-nine states in the United States, to Europe, Africa, Brazil, and Canada, and was a visiting professor at the University of the Western Cape, Cape Town, South Africa.

Dr. Lenox resides in San Diego, CA.

www.ingramcontent.com/pod-product-compliance
Lightning Source LLC
Chambersburg PA
CBHW042136160426
43200CB00019B/2951